# Gracie
## WITH GOOD NEWS FOR YOU

The C.R. Gibson Company, Norwalk, Connecticut 06856

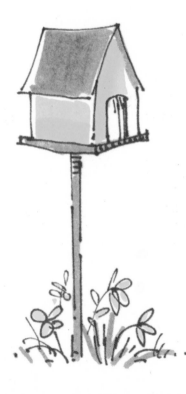

Copyright © 1987 by Anne FitzGerald and Dorothy Hall
North American edition published by
The C.R. Gibson Company
Norwalk, Connecticut 06856
All rights reserved
Co-edition arranged with the help of Angus Hudson, London
Printed in Italy
ISBN 0-8378-1830-3

# Gracie

HAS GOOD NEWS FOR YOU!
GOD KNOWS YOU BEST,
LOVES YOU MOST,
AND WILL TAKE PERFECT
CARE OF YOU
IN ALL
SITUATIONS

JUST REMEMBER···

ROMANS 8:28

ALL THINGS WORK TOGETHER
FOR GOOD ··· FOR THOSE
              WHO LOVE GOD


ALL THINGS ··· GOOD AND BAD,
                WORK TOGETHER

<u>ECCLES. 3:11</u>.

HE HATH MADE EVERYTHING
BEAUTIFUL IN HIS
              TIME

AND REMEMBER ... HIS TIMING
               IS PERFECT.

ROMANS 8:18

WHAT WE SUFFER NOW
IS NOTHING COMPARED TO THE
GLORY HE WILL GIVE US
                    LATER



AND IF HE SAYS IT
            HE MEANS IT!

## PROVERBS 16:9

WE SHOULD MAKE PLANS
KNOWING GOD WILL DIRECT
US

NO PLANS ... NO DIRECTION

<u>JOHN 16:33</u>.

BE OF GOOD CHEER:
I HAVE OVERCOME THE WORLD.



NOW ... ISN'T THAT GREAT NEWS?

PROVERBS 18:10

THE LORD IS A STRONG FORTRESS
YOU CAN RUN TO HIM
AND BE SAFE

RUN TO HIM··· YOU CAN WEAR YOURSELF
OUT RUNNING TO OTHERS

ISAIAH 40:31

THEY THAT WAIT ON THE LORD
WILL SOAR ON WINGS LIKE
EAGLES.

SEE··· YOU'LL BE ABOVE IT IN NO TIME
AT ALL!

NEH. 8:10
THE JOY OF THE LORD
IS YOUR STRENGTH.

HAVE A GOOD LAUGH...
ITS GREAT MEDICINE!

PSALM 4:8

I WILL LIE DOWN IN PEACE
AND SLEEP, FOR EVEN WHEN
I'M ALONE LORD,

YOU KEEP ME SAFE.

IT'S WONDERFUL...
HE KEEPS A 24 HOUR WATCH
OVER US !

JOHN 8:12
I AM THE LIGHT
            OF THE WORLD

SO···JUST WALK WHERE THE LIGHT IS!

## LUKE 12:28

IF THE LORD SO CLOTHES
THE GRASS WHICH IS HERE TODAY
AND GONE TOMORROW
··· HOW MUCH MORE
WILL HE CLOTHE
YOU?

OH, HOW HE LOVES AND CARES
FOR US!

PHIL. 4:6

BE ANXIOUS FOR NOTHING
BUT IN EVERYTHING BY PRAYER
LET YOUR REQUESTS
      BE MADE KNOWN
            TO GOD

WORRY ABOUT NOTHING...
      PRAY ABOUT EVERYTHING!

MORE GOOD NEWS···
GOD'S PROMISES ARE
SURE AND GOOD
FOR YESTERDAY
TODAY
AND
FOREVER

JUST REMEMBER THAT!